Managing Adverse and Reportable Information Regarding General and Flag Officers

T0308587

Margaret C. Harrell, William M. Hix

Prepared for the Office of the Secretary of Defense

NATIONAL DEFENSE RESEARCH INSTITUTE

The research described in this report was prepared for the Office of the Secretary of Defense (OSD). The research was conducted within the RAND National Defense Research Institute, a federally funded research and development center sponsored by OSD, the Joint Staff, the Unified Combatant Commands, the Navy, the Marine Corps, the defense agencies, and the defense Intelligence Community under Contract W74V8H-06-C-0002.

Library of Congress Control Number: 2012950348

ISBN: 978-0-8330-5233-9

Published 2012 by the RAND Corporation
1776 Main Street, P.O. Box 2138, Santa Monica, CA 90407-2138
1200 South Hayes Street, Arlington, VA 22202-5050
4570 Fifth Avenue, Suite 600, Pittsburgh, PA 15213-2665
RAND URL: http://www.rand.org/
To order RAND documents or to obtain additional information, contact
Distribution Services: Telephone: (310) 451-7002;
Fax: (310) 451-6915; Email: order@rand.org

Preface

Title 10 of the U.S. Code requires consideration of adverse information by all general and flag officer boards. Also, adverse information is considered within the services and by the Secretary of Defense when nominating senior officers for assignment. The Secretary of Defense must issue certifications to the President and the Senate Armed Services Committee (SASC) regarding this information. However, there is a diversity of sources and terminology used to describe events of concern and individuals involved in such events, and recent individual cases have suggested possible gaps in the processes overall. This study is intended to describe and evaluate the reporting practices of the Department of Defense (DoD) and thus ensure that consistent, reliable information supports decisions regarding the management of general and flag officers.

The processes described within are complicated and there exists no single authority. Multiple representatives from each service have reviewed the descriptions of the service processes.

This research was sponsored by the Under Secretary of Defense for Personnel and Readiness and conducted within the Forces and Resources Policy Center of the RAND National Defense Research Institute, a federally funded research and development center sponsored by the Office of the Secretary of Defense, the Joint Staff, the Unified Combatant Commands, the Navy, the Marine Corps, the defense agencies, and the defense Intelligence Community.

For more information on the RAND Forces and Resources Policy Center, see http://www.rand.org/nsrd/ndri/centers/frp.html or contact the director (contact information is provided on the web page).

Contents

Figures

Summary

Background

Adverse and reportable information must be considered at the time of assignments, promotions, or retirements of senior military officers. However, the processes for identifying and considering this information, as well as the offices and resources involved, differ across the services and are not well documented or well understood. This monograph describes these processes and identifies several potential gaps: areas where actual practice differs from the required practice, or where current practice—or the supporting data—may be inadequate to consider adverse information appropriately and completely. This document considers two categories of information: adverse and reportable. These are defined as follows:

- Adverse information: ". . . any substantiated adverse finding or conclusion from an officially documented investigation or inquiry, or other official record for report. Adverse information of a credible nature does not include information that is more than 10 years old or records of minor offenses that did not result in personal harm or significant property damage."[1]

---

[1]   Under Secretary of Defense for Personnel and Readiness (USD P&R), "General and Flag Officer Boards—Adverse Information of a Credible Nature," memorandum for Secretary of the Army, Secretary of the Navy, Secretary of the Air Force, Chairman of the Joint Chiefs of Staff, Washington, D.C., July 19, 2006.

- Reportable information: ". . . where the allegations have received significant media attention or when the Senate Armed Services Committee (SASC) brings allegations to the attention of the Department of Defense."[2]

Potential adverse information comes from multiple sources, including (but not limited to) criminal investigation files, Inspector General (IG) investigation files, equal employment opportunity (EEO) files, and equal opportunity (EO) files. Each service has an internal process to consider whether information extracted from these files qualifies as adverse information.

Personnel Processes

The personnel processes of interest that consider adverse and reportable information include promotion to O-7 and to O-8, promotion to and assignment for O-9 and O-10, and retirement from general and flag officer ranks.[3]

In the case of promotion to O-7 and O-8, adverse information must be considered by a promotion selection board. If adverse information for a newly selected officer is discovered after the promotion selection board, that information must be considered by a promotion review board, which recommends to the secretary of the military department whether to support that individual's promotion. The promotion selection board's chair and the service secretary must certify exemplary conduct of all selected officers. In the case of individuals with adverse or reportable information that has not previously been considered by the Senate, DoD must acknowledge and describe the information to the President and the Senate. Officers promoted to O-8 must also com-

---

[2]   Department of Defense Instruction (DoDI) 1320.4, *Military Officer Actions Requiring Approval of the Secretary of Defense or the President, or Confirmation by the Senate*, March 14, 1995.

[3]   These processes are described in Chapter Three.

plete a financial disclosure, which identifies any conflict of interest or financial information of concern.

When officers are recommended for an O-9 or O-10 assignment, whether or not the assignment involves a promotion, adverse and reportable information must be acknowledged and described. In most services, any existing adverse information is considered when the service recommends an officer for an assignment. In all cases, adverse and reportable information that has not previously been considered by the Senate must be clearly described and acknowledged as part of the nomination package. Further, individual officers must complete a financial disclosure and must also complete a questionnaire from the SASC that addresses prior misconduct. This information is considered by the Senate during the confirmation process.

The consideration of adverse and reportable information on the occasion of retirement from general and flag officer ranks differs slightly from consideration during the assignment and promotion processes. Retirement does not require Senate confirmation. The service secretary can approve retirements from the grades of O-7 and O-8; the Secretary of Defense has the authority to approve retirements from the grades of O-9 and O-10. The Secretary of Defense certifies to the President and the Senate that the retiring officer served satisfactorily in grade. The scope of the inquiries for adverse information also differs for retirement, as the focus is on the current grade rather than the ten years preceding the personnel action.

Evaluation and Discussion

This monograph includes several observations about the personnel processes that consider adverse and reportable information. These are summarized below.

Documented Guidance Is Incomplete or Requires Revision

The DoD instruction governing these processes (DoDI 1320.4) is supplemented by memoranda that should be incorporated into the instruction. Additionally, the instruction could be revised to provide a clear definition of reportable information and to refer to both EEO and EO. The companion Chairman of the Joint Chiefs of Staff (CJCS) instruction (CJCSI 1331.01D) is inconsistent with the current DoD requirements. The services have their own written guidance. Some of these documents provide robust description of parts of the process, but no service has complete documented guidance about the assignment, promotion, and retirement processes for all general and flag officers.

The Services' Processes Differ, and There Is No Expert in the Process

The services' processes differ regarding the roles of the offices involved. As long as adverse and reportable information is managed consistently across the services, there appears to be no compelling reason that the services' processes or offices involved should be the same.

However, each service's process involves many different offices and individuals in the process, including (but not limited to) the general and flag officer management offices, offices responsible for officer management below the ranks of general and flag officer, the IG, the judge advocate general, general counsel, and those offices that manage additional data files, such as EO, EEO, and criminal investigations. In no service is there an individual with either expert knowledge of the entire process or responsibility for the entire process.

There Are Gaps in the EEO and EO Processes and the Data That Support Those Processes

At the time of this study, the services were not consistently checking both EO and EEO files consistent with the requirements to identify adverse information. Additionally, the EO and EEO data available in the services were insufficient to conduct such checks properly. This occurred in part, but not entirely, because those involved in general and flag officer processes did not always clearly understand the difference between EEO and EO.

Department of Defense Inspector General Screens Are Inconsistently Requested

Although the Department of Defense Inspector General (DoD IG) files must be queried both before and after selection boards, the services were not consistently doing so prior to O-7 selection boards.

The Amount of Information Provided to Selection Boards Varies; That Provided to Promotion Review Boards Is Lacking in Detail

Promotion selection boards are required to consider any adverse information. The summaries of such information provided to the selection boards tend to be approximately one page in length. The amount of information provided to promotion review boards varies: Some promotion review boards see the same type of one-page summary that would be shown to a selection board; some see redacted reports of investigation (ROIs) that are often seven to ten pages in length; some see complete investigative files, including, but not limited to, nonredacted ROIs.

There Is Greater Focus on the Assignment and Promotion Processes Than on the Retirement Process

DoD and the SASC focus primarily on assignment and promotion processes, rather than on the retirement process. This seems appropriate for two reasons. First, the retirement process only considers adverse and reportable information occurring within the officer's current pay grade. Further, the retirement process does not require Senate confirmation.

DoD and the SASC Have Different Philosophies About the Process

DoD and the SASC perceive these processes differently, and these differences are evident in several ways.

First, DoD defines and treats adverse information as an incident. In contrast, the SASC has expressed interest in the overall individual, with special emphasis on the judgment of the individual. The DoD process, and especially the IG processes within DoD, do not focus on an individual's judgment. DoD and the SASC also have both different thresholds of information required and different timelines.

Many senior officers in the services feel strongly that senior officers should have the opportunity and the authority and discretion to privately counsel officers, for their professional development. Such counseling may result in documentation, such as nonpunitive letters of communication. The SASC would like to see these documents, whereas the services maintain that those are private documents.

Additionally, the DoD definition of adverse information is limited to incidents within the past ten years, whereas the SASC asks officers nominated for O-9 and O-10 assignments to provide information about any adverse incident, without limiting the request to ten years.

Another difference is their perspectives on the scrutiny that should apply to officers of different pay grades; SASC staff expressed a view that more senior officers should endure more scrutiny, but the DoD system applies the same standards of adverse information to all officers. Also, increased scrutiny would suggest that adverse information that did not hinder promotion to O-7 might be of concern for subsequent nominations, but the current processes do not revisit adverse information that was considered by the SASC during a prior personnel action.

Finally, SASC staff believe that the services should consider each adverse case in more depth and should read all supporting investigative materials, whereas service personnel typically determine which cases require a thorough reading, without presuming the need to read all investigative materials for all adverse cases.

Recommendations

The recommendations that emerged from this RAND analysis are discussed in more detail in the final chapter of this monograph and include the following:

- The Office of the Secretary of Defense and the Joint Staff should update DoD and Joint Staff guidance.
- These guidance documents should clarify the definition of reportable information and the means by which the list of reportable

information will be updated and distributed to the general and flag officer management offices.

- The services should clarify, with formal service directives or instructions, the processes by which adverse and reportable information is considered in general and flag officer personnel processes.
- Each service should identify the individual within the service who is responsible for the entire nomination and retirement process, including the inclusion of adverse and reportable information.
- The services should ensure that they satisfy the requirement to prescreen all officers eligible for promotion to pay grades O-7 and O-8 and that the prescreens include DoD IG checks.
- The services should provide complete investigative materials to promotion review boards.
- Law and regulations should retain the opportunity for the services to privately counsel officers without risk of the incident being considered in a nomination.
- The SASC and DoD should initiate a dialog and recognize the differences between the DoD and the SASC perspectives regarding adverse information processes, especially pertaining to levels of scrutiny and issues of individual judgment.
- Service personnel should read the complete investigative materials of each case unless they explicitly determine the individual case does *not* require a complete reading.

Acknowledgments

The authors appreciate the sponsor support provided by William Carr, Lernes Hebert, Cheryl Black, and COL Marsha Curtis from the Office of the Under Secretary of Defense for Personnel and Readiness, Officer and Enlisted Personnel Management, and by Donald M. Horstman, Kristopher Miltner, and Leo FitzHarris, Office of the DoD Inspector General. We thank Gary Leeling and Dick Walsh for their time and willingness to convey the Senate Armed Services Committee perspective. The research contained in this monograph and the accompanying appendix document reflects the exceptional cooperation and participation of many individuals from the Office of the Secretary of Defense, the Joint Staff, and each service. The authors appreciate the willingness of many individuals to participate in discussion sessions and would like especially to thank those who provided substantive input to our research: James Smyser (DoD Office of the General Counsel); Col John Doucette (Joint Staff); Andrew Bevil, Henry Finley, CW3 Billy Frittz, COL Michael Erdley, LTC Lyndon Johnson, Daniel McCallum, MG William H. McCoy, and Dashana Taylor (Army); CDR George Bradshaw, Stephen Coyle, David Dillensnyder, Robert Erskine, William Kellum, CAPT Gary Sharp, John Shea, LCDR Colleen Shook, and LT John Woods (Navy); Kevin McHenka, Alan K. Passey, Lt Col Peter Renner, Paul Sandy, Col Thomas Sharpy, and Lt Col Charlie Underhill (Air Force); and Capt. Adam Brill, Cynthia Edwards, Alfrita Jones, Capt. Ji Kwon, LtCol. Eric Larson, Rita Looney, LtCol. Eric Lyon, LtCol. William Redman, and Virgil White (Marine Corps). We also appreciate the input of Diana Donnelly and George

Mulligan from the White House Military Office. This project benefited from contributions from RAND colleagues Gary Cecchine and Rena Rudovsky, as well as from RAND military fellow LCDR Daniel Cobian. This monograph and the accompanying appendix document were improved by RAND peer reviewers Lawrence Hanser and Harry Thie and RAND research editor James Torr.

Abbreviations

CIDC	U.S. Army Criminal Investigation Command
COCOM	combatant command
CJCS	Chairman of the Joint Chiefs of Staff
CJCSI	Chairman of the Joint Chiefs of Staff instruction
CPMS	Civilian Personnel Management Service
DoD	U.S. Department of Defense
DoDD	Department of Defense Directive
DoDI	Department of Defense instruction
DoD IG	Department of Defense Inspector General
EEO	equal employment opportunity
EEOC	Equal Employment Opportunity Commission
EO	equal opportunity
GOMO	General Officer Management Office; used generically herein to indicate that office in each of the services
IG	inspector general
JAG	judge advocate general
NCIS	Naval Criminal Investigative Service
NPLC	non-punitive letter of communication
OSD	Office of the Secretary of Defense
OSI	Air Force Office of Special Investigations

OUSD P&R	Office of the Under Secretary of Defense for Personnel and Readiness
PRB	promotion review board
RMO	responsible management official
ROI	report of investigation
SASC	Senate Armed Services Committee
SF 278	Standard Form 278, Public Financial Disclosure Report
TIG	time in grade
USD P&R	Under Secretary of Defense for Personnel and Readiness

CHAPTER ONE

Introduction

This monograph documents the Department of Defense (DoD) and service policies and practices surrounding the identification and consideration of adverse and reportable information on senior military officials being considered for personnel actions requiring approval of the President or confirmation by the Senate. This work identifies several potential gaps: areas where actual practice differs from the required practice, or where current practice—or the supporting data—may be inadequate to consider adverse information appropriately and completely. The personnel actions of interest consist of promotions to one- and two-star ranks (pay grades O-7 and O-8), nominations for three- and four-star (pay grades O-9 and O-10) appointments and promotions, and retirements at all general officer grades.

The current definitions of adverse and reportable information are as follows:

- Adverse information: ". . . any substantiated adverse finding or conclusion from an officially documented investigation or inquiry, or other official record for report. Adverse information of a credible nature does not include information that is more than 10 years old or records of minor offenses that did not result in personal harm or significant property damage."[1]

---

[1]   Under Secretary of Defense for Personnel and Readiness (USD P&R), "General and Flag Officer Boards—Adverse Information of a Credible Nature," memorandum for Secretary of the Army, Secretary of the Navy, Secretary of the Air Force, Chairman of the Joint Chiefs of Staff, Washington, D.C., July 19, 2006.

- Reportable information: ". . . where the allegations have received significant media attention or when the Senate Armed Services Committee (SASC) brings allegations to the attention of the Department of Defense."[2]

The Office of the Under Secretary of Defense for Personnel and Readiness (OUSD P&R) requested the study, citing continuing concerns on the part of both SASC personnel and Office of the Secretary of Defense (OSD) officials about the thoroughness, completeness, and consistency with law and regulations of service and DoD practices and policies surrounding the gathering and reporting of adverse information.

While, in general, both OSD personnel and SASC staff suggest that policies and procedures seem generally appropriate and improved over the past several years, they mention that lapses in reporting and differences in opinion regarding information appropriate to report, from a service either to DoD or to the SASC, still occur from time to time. Further, the details of each service process are not available in a comprehensive document.[3] Hence, it has previously been difficult to evaluate existing policies and practices.

Research Approach

This research describes the current practices for considering adverse and reportable information during assignment, promotion, and retirement processes for general and flag officers. The purpose of this research is to

---

[2]   Department of Defense Instruction (DoDI) 1320.4, *Military Officer Actions Requiring Approval of the Secretary of Defense or the President, or Confirmation by the Senate*, March 14, 1995.

[3]   Of the four services, the Army has the most complete documentation of its process, captured in U.S. Department of the Army, Secretary of the Army, "Policy Concerning Adverse Information for Officers Being Considered for Promotion, Appointment, or Federal Recognition of a General Officer Grade," January 22, 2007, not available to the general public. Nevertheless, the memorandum still lacks a description of some of the details that are required in the process.

evaluate and discuss the extent to which these practices, and the data that support them, sufficiently consider adverse and reportable information, consistent with law, DoD and service guidance, and SASC expectations.

This research is based on review of the policy guidance as well as on the data from multiple individual and group interviews with participants representing each of the military services, OSD, and SASC staff. We developed the process descriptions described herein through these interviews, not by directly following an individual nomination with adverse information. We completed multiple interviews regarding each aspect of the process, to ensure that we spoke directly with the individual responsible for each aspect of the process. Some of the interviews were conducted personally, whereas others were conducted by telephone. We do not cite the individual sources of this information, who spoke on behalf of their organizations. Nor do we attribute information specifically to individual services. Instead, this information is relayed from a DoD-wide perspective, with the intent of describing the processes and identifying gaps in the processes but without attributing gaps to a particular service.

This material has been presented in a briefing, which has been viewed and commented on by representatives from each service. Additionally, service representatives had the opportunity to comment on a draft report.

Organization of This Monograph

Chapter Two describes the circumstances leading to the current requirements for the consideration of adverse and reportable information during promotion, assignment, and retirement processes, and provides those requirements. Chapter Three documents the current processes for considering adverse information during promotion to O-7 and O-8, assignment and promotion for O-9 and O-10 officers, and retirement of general and flag officers. Chapter Four provides discussion and evaluation. The final chapter includes recommendations.

CHAPTER TWO

Background

Before describing and evaluating current adverse information practices, it is useful to describe the background of events that contributed to the current policies and the requirements for general and flag officer personnel processes.

The current set of DoD and service policies surrounding the consideration of adverse information attendant to personnel actions on general and flag officers can be traced to a specific situation with an Army general officer in 1988. At that time, the regulation governing officer actions requiring approval of the President, the Secretary of Defense, or confirmation by the Senate, DoDI 1320.4, dated October 29, 1981, made no mention whatsoever of adverse information or any requirement to report it along with nomination packages.[1]

The 1988 Incident

In August 1988, Senators Sam Nunn and John Warner, the chair and ranking minority member of the SASC, respectively, co-signed a letter to Secretary of Defense Frank Carlucci expressing their "deep concern" over the recent retirement of a particular Army lieutenant general.[2] According to the letter, several weeks after the Senate had confirmed

---

[1] The 1981 version of DoDI 1320.4 remained in effect until the current 1995 version was promulgated.

[2] U.S. Senate, Committee on Armed Services, "Letter to the Honorable Frank Carlucci," signed by Sam Nunn and John W. Warner, Washington, D.C., August 1, 1988.

the officer's retirement (in June 1988) in the grade of lieutenant general, the committee received information that in March of that year, the Army had disciplined the officer for improper use of government transportation and unauthorized release of sensitive information to a government contractor, facts that the senators felt "cast doubt on the propriety" of the officer's retirement in grade and would have been material to the decision to confirm the officer's retirement as a lieutenant general. Although the officer had received a letter of reprimand in March, before the President signed and forwarded the nomination to the Senate in May, no mention of it was made in the President's nomination package.

The senators' letter asked the Secretary (1) why the committee was not notified of the adverse information until after the confirmation, (2) who decided to withhold the information from the committee, (3) whether any further action was anticipated against the officer and whether the Justice Department had been advised of the officer's offenses, and (4) what actions the Secretary intended to take to bring necessary information to the attention of the committee in the future. Finally, the letter asked that until further notice "all flag and general officer nominations be accompanied by a statement regarding any adverse action taken or pending against the officer since his or her last Senate confirmation." A summary of relevant facts associated with any adverse information was to accompany the nomination.

After an exchange of letters with Senators Nunn and Warner, in September of 1988 the Secretary set forth a new policy. He instructed the secretaries of the military departments to include in all future three- and four-star nominations the following statement:

> Investigative files and all systems of records maintained in the Department referring to this officer by name or identifying particulars, including Standard Form 278 (Financial Disclosure Report), have been reviewed, and we find no evidence of conflict of interest or failure to adhere to required standards of conduct. Additionally, there is no evidence of misconduct nor is there, to

my knowledge, a pending investigation of alleged misconduct by this officer.[3]

Future one- and two-star nominations were to include a similar statement, excluding reference to the Standard Form 278, Public Financial Disclosure Report (SF 278), for one-star nominations, as the financial disclosure form is not required for personnel actions at that grade.

Finally, in the memorandum the Secretary directed each military department to

> . . . update internal procedures as necessary to ensure that all available investigative files and record systems (including those of the Inspector General, Judge Advocate General, Defense Criminal Investigative Service and other appropriate activities) are included in this review.

This policy was formalized in a March 1995 revision to DoDI 1320.4, as follows:

> 6.1.1.2. The Secretaries of the Military Departments shall ensure that all investigative files, to include Equal Employment Opportunity files, are reviewed prior to forwarding a nomination to the Secretary of Defense for GFO [general and flag officer] actions requiring approval by the Secretary of Defense or the President, or confirmation by the Senate. Based on those reviews, the Secretaries of the Military Departments shall forward through the Chairman of the Joint Chiefs of Staff any adverse information as prescribed in paragraph 6.2., below, or, if no adverse information, make the following certification:

---

[3]   Secretary of Defense, "General and Flag Officer Nominations," memorandum for the Secretary of the Army, Washington, D.C., September 2, 1988. Because the text of the memorandum to the Secretary of the Army directs "each Military Department" to update their internal procedures, one can assume that similar, if not identical, letters went to each service secretary.

6.1.1.2.1. All systems of records, to include Equal Employment Opportunity files and Standard Form 278 (Public Financial Disclosure Report)[Delete SF 278 reference for one star nominations], maintained in the Department of Defense that pertain to this/these officer(s) have been examined. The files contain no adverse information about this/these officer(s) since his/her/their last Senate confirmation. Further, to the best of my knowledge, there is no planned or ongoing investigation or inquiry into matters that constitute alleged adverse information on the part of this/these officer(s).[4]

This 1995 policy on provision of adverse information through the chain to the Senate remains in force today, with some modifications in memoranda. For example, a July 19, 2006, memorandum defined adverse information of a credible nature more precisely as

[a]ny substantiated adverse finding or conclusion from an officially documented investigation or inquiry *or any other official record or report. Adverse information of a credible nature does not include information that is more than 10 years old or records of minor offenses that did not result in personal harm or significant property damage.* (Italics added to indicate revisions to the original definition.)[5]

Interviews with DoD officials and Senate staff responsible for the process report that, with occasional lapses, the policy seems to be generally working well and that, with periodic exceptions, a significant degree of trust now exists between the department and the SASC. Subsequent chapters of this monograph offer more detail on the current policy and remaining issues with both the policy and its execution.

---

[4]   DoDI 1320.4, p. 3.

[5]   USD P&R, "General and Flag Officer Boards—Adverse Information of a Credible Nature," memorandum for Secretary of the Army, Secretary of the Navy, Secretary of the Air Force, Chairman of the Joint Chiefs of Staff, Washington, D.C., July 19, 2006.

Information Provided to Promotion Boards

In addition to the above policy surrounding the provision of adverse information up the chain after senior officers have been selected for personnel actions, there has been an evolution of policy dealing with adverse information considered during the selection process. Specifically, this second policy pertains to information provided to one- and two-star promotion boards and to selecting officials in the case of three- and four-star nominations for promotion or assignment, and for retirement in all general and flag officer grades.

In 2003, USD P&R made the Deputy Secretary of Defense aware that the military departments employed differing policies on pre-board screening for adverse information. According to an internal 2003 DoD memorandum,[6] at that time neither the Navy nor the Marine Corps conducted any pre-board screening. For brigadier general boards, the Army screened only the "top contenders," about 15 percent of those eligible, while the Air Force screened all those eligible. The Army included all DoD investigative agencies in its screening, whereas the Air Force excluded the DoD Inspector General (DoD IG) from its checks. For promotion to major general, the two services screened 100 percent of eligibles and with all DoD agencies. This varied set of policies was confusing to the SASC as well as those inside DoD; it was not clear what data were being checked for which officers. These differences also raised questions of fairness.

Until 2006, there was no statutory or regulatory requirement for adverse information other than that contained in an officer's official military personnel file to be considered by promotion selection boards. The Fiscal Year 2006 National Defense Authorization Act amended Title 10 of the U.S. Code to require that adverse information of a credible nature, including any substantiated finding or conclusion from an officially documented investigation or inquiry, be provided to general

---

[6]   USD P&R, "Managing Adverse Information," memorandum for the Deputy Secretary of Defense, Washington, D.C., January 31, 2003.

and flag officer promotion boards.[7] DoD implemented the legislative requirement by promulgating appropriate changes to DoDI 1320.4 and DoDI 1320.14.[8] In addition to requiring all adverse information of a credible nature to be shown to promotion selection boards, the change to DoDI 1320.14 required any such information not available in time to be shown to the promotion selection board to be shown to a subsequent promotion review board (PRB) before the secretary of the military department concerned decides whether to support a selected officer for promotion.

According to the memorandum announcing the new policy, the change was precipitated by several instances in which the various military departments had sent forward nomination packages for promotion of officers about whom adverse information had come to light that had not been considered by promotion selection boards.

Summary of Current Requirements

Currently, the statutory and regulatory requirements surrounding reporting of adverse and related information vary by grade.

O-7 and O-8 Promotion and Assignment Requirements

For officers nominated for promotion to O-7 and O-8, promotion selection boards are required to see any credible adverse information available at the time of the convening of the board.[9] Any credible adverse information that becomes known after the board convenes must go before a PRB.[10] In addition, promotion selection board chairs and ser-

---

[7]   Enacted as Public Law 109-163. The relevant section is 506. The law modified sections 615(a)(3) and 14107(a)(3) of Title 10, which pertain to active and reserve component officers, respectively.

[8]   USD P&R, July 19, 2006.

[9]   This requirement was part of the National Defense Authorization Act for 2006.

[10]   This requirement is not statutory but is the result of an informal agreement between OSD and the staff of the SASC, codified in DoDI 1320.14, *Commissioned Officer Promotion Program Procedures*, September 24, 1996.

vice secretaries must certify exemplary conduct of all officers selected.[11] Officers selected for O-8 must also complete SF 278.

O-9 and O-10 Promotion and Assignment Requirements

Service secretaries must certify exemplary conduct, as with O-7 and O-8s, for all officers nominated for appointment to positions in the grade of O-9 and O-10, but the board requirements do not exist, as there are no boards for these more senior appointments. Nominees must also complete a SASC questionnaire and SF 278.

All General and Flag Officer Promotions and Appointments

Service secretaries must either provide any credible adverse information or certify than none exists.[12]

O-7 and O-8 Retirement Requirements

Service secretaries or under secretaries may approve all retirements from the pay grades O-7 and O-8 that do not require a time-in-grade (TIG) waiver. Those retirements may not be approved unless the officer has been checked against all investigative and personnel files, including equal employment opportunity (EEO) files and DoD IG files.[13] USD P&R must approve all O-7 and O-8 retirements with TIG waivers.

O-9 and O-10 Retirement Requirements

USD P&R has the authority, delegated from the Secretary of Defense, to approve O-9 and O-10 retirements of individuals that do not have adverse or reportable information and that do not require TIG waivers. Service secretaries must provide a substantive basis for recommending

---

[11] USD P&R, "Officer Appointments—Exemplary Conduct," memorandum for Secretary of the Army, Secretary of the Navy, Secretary of the Air Force, Chairman of the Joint Chiefs of Staff, Washington, D.C., February 12, 2007.

[12] Per DoDI 1320.4.

[13] Secretary of Defense, "Processing Retirement Applications of Officers in the Grades of O-7 and O-8," memorandum for Secretary of the Army, Secretary of the Navy, Secretary of the Air Force, Undersecretary of Defense (Personnel and Readiness), General Counsel (DoD), Inspector General (DoD), Washington, D.C., October 19, 1998.

that the Secretary of Defense or USD P&R certify satisfactory service in that pay grade.[14]

The Current Situation

Since 2006, policies associated with the handling of adverse information have remained essentially stable. Occasional issues arise as senators or committee staff learn of possible adverse information that DoD has not provided with nomination packages. Similarly, OSD sometimes learns of such information not provided by a military department, and these instances sometimes cause concern about the overall processes.

The principal purpose of the remainder of this monograph is to describe the processes dealing with adverse and reportable information attendant to promotion, appointment, and retirement of general and flag officers. Further, the monograph offers observations about the strengths and shortcomings of those processes. It is our intent that these observations will improve the processes and, in the end, enhance the trust and confidence of all concerned in those processes and those who conduct them.

---

[14] USD P&R, "Memorandum Provides Instructions for the Processing of Three- and Four-Star Retirement Recommendations," memorandum for Secretary of the Army, Secretary of the Navy, Secretary of the Air Force, Chairman of the Joint Chiefs of Staff, Washington, D.C., June 21, 1996.

CHAPTER THREE

Personnel Processes

Preceding the Selection Board for Promotion to O-7 and O-8

Figure 3.1 shows the process preceding the selection board for promotion to O-7 and O-8. The discussion below describes that process.

The process for promotion to O-7 and O-8 begins for all services with a determination of the promotion zone and thus a deter-

Figure 3.1
Preceding O-7 and O-8 Selection Boards

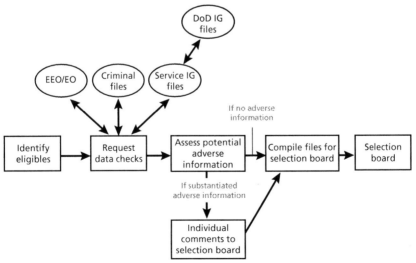

NOTES: EEO = equal employment opportunity; EO = equal opportunity; IG = Inspector General.
RAND *MG1088-3.1*

mination of the officers eligible for promotion. Under the Fiscal Year 2006 National Defense Authorization Act and a July 2006 memorandum signed by USD P&R, there has been a requirement "that adverse information of a credible nature, including any substantiated adverse finding or conclusion from an officially documented investigation or inquiry, be provided to general and flag officer promotion selection boards" and to federal recognition boards.[1]

As a result, each service conducts pre-board screenings of officers who have been identified as candidates for promotion. This is indicated in the second box of Figure 3.1, which is connected to the ovals indicating the types of data that are required to be checked: EO/EEO, criminal data files, and IG files from both the service and the DoD IG.[2] All services review their respective IG files and criminal investigation files. One service has stated concerns that its centralized IG database is not robust for years prior to 2008, but it is currently addressing this shortcoming.

Generally there is a single office in the services responsible for coordinating the systems of records checks for the pre-board screenings, but not all screenings are requested by that office or are returned directly to that office. For example, the IG in one service requests and receives the screenings, as does the personnel office in another service. However, in one service, the promotions office requests the records checks, and receives most of them, except for the criminal investigations screenings. In that service, the criminal investigations screenings are sent directly to the judge advocate general (JAG), where the promotions office also sends the other completed pre-board screenings.

This analysis suggests, however, that the data from the checks are more important than which offices request and receive the data checks. Indeed, the data considered for the pre-board screenings vary

---

[1]   USD P&R, July 19, 2006.

[2]   EO/EEO and criminal data are checked within the military department. Criminal data are maintained by the U.S. Army Criminal Investigation Command (CIDC), Naval Criminal Investigative Service (NCIS), and the Air Force Office of Special Investigations (OSI). EO and EEO differ in that EO cases are those with a military victim or complainant and EEO cases involve a civilian victim or complainant. EEO and EO are discussed in greater detail in Chapter Four.

somewhat. As mentioned, all services review their respective IG files and criminal investigation files. However, currently only two services request pre-board checks from the DoD IG.[3] There are also differences in the EEO and EO checks requested from each service. One service checks both EEO and EO files prior to the selection board. Two services check EEO but not EO data. The remaining service conducts neither EEO nor EO checks prior to the selection board.[4]

Additionally, one service screens names through the central clearance facility, which has the result of investigations conducted for security clearance reasons, and another service also checks a database to confirm that the individual was not declined a security clearance.

When the results from the systems of records checks return to the coordinating office, the coordinating office considers the data received to determine whether the information qualifies as adverse and thus needs to be shown to the selection board. This is represented by the third box in Figure 3.1, "Assess potential adverse information." In some instances, the information clearly falls below the threshold for the definition of adverse. Often this is because the potential adverse information does not satisfy the definition of the revised DoDI 1320.4, as it is greater than ten years old or it was a minor offense that did not result in personal harm or significant property damage. Ongoing investigations are also disregarded, as they are not presented to the selection board.

To conclude whether potentially adverse information qualifies as adverse information, each service follows a different process, but they have some commonality. All services involve senior personnel in the review of the information, which is generally in the form of a summary composed by the coordinating office.[5]

Two services employ a sequential decision process; a package containing the summaries of potentially adverse information for all officers is sent to general and flag officers as well as to senior civilian officials, who comment on each case and send the file to the next decisionmaker.

---

[3]   This is discussed in greater detail in Chapter Four.

[4]   EO and EEO are discussed in more detail in Chapter Four.

[5]   This process involves generals or flag officers senior to the officer with potentially adverse information.

All services permit individual officers with potentially adverse information to comment on the information before a decision is made regarding whether the information is adverse. The services vary in the manner in which the individual officer is informed, however. In most cases, the potentially adverse information is communicated directly to the individual officer, although one service communicates through the officer's chain of command. The officer's comments are considered in the deliberation of the information.

If the information is substantiated as adverse, the individual is permitted to provide comment to the selection board.[6] One service includes any supporting information provided by the individual officer in their file for the selection board. On the occasion that adverse information is communicated to the selection board, the amount of information provided is relatively brief; it is generally provided as a one-page summary. The services do not share a common format for providing adverse information to the selection board.

Following the O-7 and O-8 Selection Board

Figure 3.2 indicates the process following the selection board.

Screening After the Selection Board

Immediately after the selection board is complete, the services begin the post-selection screening process. The offices that initiate these screenings vary across the services. In two services, the general officer management office (GOMO)[7] office does so; in the other services, the JAG or IG offices do so. These screenings involve the same in-service data checks that were completed prior to the selection boards.[8] Like-

---

[6]   All officers have the opportunity to communicate information directly to a promotion selection board.

[7]   For ease of reading, we use this abbreviation throughout this monograph to refer to the office in each of the services that manages their general or flag officers, including the Navy Flag Officer Management and Distribution Office, the Air Force General Officer Management (DPG), and the Marine Corps Senior Leader Management Branch (MMSL).

[8]   Although the DoD definition of adverse information limits the information of interest to that within the prior ten years, one service requests any adverse information from the post-selection board data inquiries, without regard for the ten-year time limit.

Figure 3.2
Following O-7 and O-8 Selection Boards

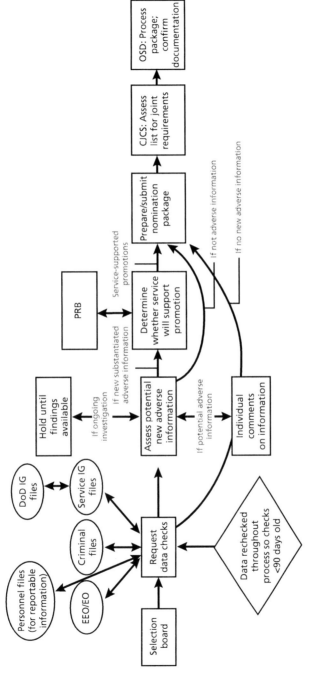

wise, all services now check EO, EEO, or both.[9] All four services also request post-selection board checks from the DoD IG. Additionally, the services now check the selectees' personnel records for reportable information.[10] The selection board is not required to consider reportable information, so this is the first time in the process that this additional information is considered. The post-selection vetting process is done repeatedly, so as to remain current within 90 days, until the selections are confirmed. Additionally, the services also have processes in place such that the service IG will inform the appropriate offices if investigations arise regarding those individuals, without waiting for the recurring check.

Managing Adverse Information

There are three types of adverse information to be managed after the selection board: (1) substantiated adverse information that was known by the selection board; (2) new information that has become apparent since the selection board and was thus not considered by it; and (3) unsubstantiated adverse information, such as allegations from an ongoing investigation.[11] The latter two would not have been presented to the selection board.

If any new information that is potentially adverse arises from these data checks, the services proceed through their processes to determine whether the information qualifies as adverse information. Although the process to make this determination varies by service, each service uses the same process that they would have used prior to the selection board for officers with potentially adverse information. This process

---

[9]   EO and EEO checks are discussed in more detail in Chapter Four. EEO and EO should both be checked both prior to and following the selection board. One service checks neither EEO nor EO prior to the selection boards and checks only EO data following the selection boards.

[10]   Reportable information includes instances where "allegations that have received significant media attention or when the Senate Armed Service [sic] Committee (SASC) brings allegations to the attention of the Department of Defense," DoDI 1320.4, March 14, 1995.

[11]   If a completed investigation concludes that the allegations are unsubstantiated, then that information is not of interest.

includes permitting the officer the chance to comment on the potentially adverse information.

In the case of unsubstantiated adverse information, such as allegations that are still under investigation, the service may choose to withhold that individual from the selection list so that the remainder of the selectees can proceed through the process while the investigation is completed. In some circumstances where a service expects the potential adverse information to be resolved quickly, it may choose to delay the entire list rather than withhold a name.

In the event that substantiated adverse information was not identified or available prior to the selection boards, the revised DoDI requires the secretary of the military department to convene a PRB consisting of three officers senior to the officer involved, which will make a recommendation to the secretary of the military department regarding whether to support the officer's promotion. The PRB process does not reflect a statutory requirement. Instead, Congress has provided tacit agreement in support of PRBs so that a board of officers can review the adverse information of an individual selected for promotion. The alternative to the PRB process would be for an officer to be considered by the subsequent promotion selection board.

In the case of substantiated adverse information, the PRB is convened, considers the adverse information, and recommends to the service secretary whether or not to support the individual's promotion. While all services conduct PRBs, the services vary in the amount of information that they provide to the PRB for consideration. One service provides the entire file of investigative materials, including the report of investigation (ROI) and supporting files, to the PRB. One service decides on a case-by-case basis whether to provide a one-page summary or more information. In the case of more information, this service provides a redacted ROI (approximately 7–10 pages). One service has shifted from providing a one-page summary to providing a package containing the redacted ROI, the officer's response, and a copy of the command response (e.g., memorandum). The fourth service has conducted very few PRBs and does not have institutional knowledge of the material provided to them.

If the service secretary subsequently decides to support the individual, then the nomination materials must include detailed information regarding the allegations (such as the ROI, in the case of an IG investigation), a summary of the adverse information, and a statement of support from the service secretary indicating the secretary's acknowledgment of the adverse information and a "specific rationale for support of the officer" as well as "a statement about how the officer meets the requirements of exemplary conduct" and thus the secretary's continued support of the selection for promotion.[12] These same documents are provided for individuals who were selected for promotion despite adverse information that was available to the selection board.

If the service secretary chooses not to support an individual selected for promotion, the service secretary can recommend that a name be removed from the promotion list. However, only the President can remove a name.

Processing the Nomination Materials

Once the services have compiled the materials required for each of the selectees, the nomination package is forwarded to the Joint Staff. The Chairman is required by law to review selection board results, largely to ensure appropriate consideration of officers serving in, or who have served in, joint assignments.[13] The Joint Staff General/Flag Officer Matters office is primarily involved in this process, and pre-coordination between the services and the Joint Staff General/Flag Officer Matters Office is recommended and customary prior to the formal transmittal of materials from the service secretary to the Chairman's office.[14] Written guidance from CJCS 1331.01D describes the nomination package as including the following:

---

[12] DoDI 1320.4; USD P&R, February 12, 2007.

[13] Chairman of the Joint Chiefs of Staf Instruction (CJCSI) 1330.02A, *Review of Promotion Selection Board Results by the Chairman of the Joint Chiefs of Staff*, May 1, 1997.

[14] CJCSI 1331.01D, *Manpower and Personnel Actions Involving General and Flag Officers*, August 1, 2010, p. E-5.

1. a memorandum from the service secretary addressing any significant aspects of the list of selectees, including any promotion objectives that were not met or any waiver requests
2. the selection board report
3. list of officers considered who currently or previously served on the Joint Staff
4. selection board joint statistics
5. résumés of officers selected
6. chairman's letter designating the joint representative
7. joint duty assignment waivers requested
8. adverse information summaries and ROIs for officers with adverse information
9. scroll, for the President's signature[15]
10. press release
11. current IG check, not more than 90 days old.[16]

The Chairman reviews the materials to determine whether the selection board was conducted in accordance with law. After reviewing the materials, the Chairman returns the report to the secretary of the military department and may support the selection board results or require additional actions, including convening a special selection board.[17]

The services submit the promotion lists to OSD. First, the OSD Correspondence Analysis Branch confirms that the appropriate scrolls, nominations, and press releases are contained in the package and have been prepared correctly. The package proceeds from there onward to OUSD P&R, where staff conduct an administrative review of the packet. This administrative review includes confirming that names and biographies are consistent throughout the materials and confirming that the IG checks are current. At this time, OUSD P&R person-

---

[15] The scroll is the document that the President signs and forwards to Congress.

[16] This requirement was revised, to 90 days rather than 60 days, in August 2010, to be consistent with the OSD requirement. However, the CJCSI still does not specify that a DoD IG check, rather than just a service IG check, is required.

[17] CJCSI 1331.01D, pp. E6–E7.

nel also review the promotion board statistics regarding race, gender, acquisition personnel, and joint qualifications. OUSD P&R staff may consult with the DoD EO office, or with the Under Secretary of Defense for Acquisition, Technology and Logistics regarding these statistics. OUSD P&R personnel will also confirm that, should the selectees include any individuals with adverse information, sufficient and correct documentation is included in the package regarding that information.

When the administrative review is complete, the package proceeds to the OSD General Counsel for review and return for review by OUSD P&R.

Differences Between O-7 and O-8 Promotion

This discussion has addressed both O-7 and O-8 selection and promotion processes. However, while promotion to O-7 and to O-8 follows roughly the same process in each service, there are some differences between the processes for promotion to O-7 and those for promotion to O-8. One difference is that different offices are involved in the process for some services. For example, the service offices that manage officers at the pay grades of O-6 and below tend to be involved in both the determination of eligible officers for promotion to O-7 and also in the requests for data checks prior to the O-7 selection board. Following selection to O-7 and throughout the O-8 selection process, those offices responsible for managing general and flag officers are more involved.

Additionally, the promotion process to O-8 is less burdensome, both because there are many fewer officers eligible for promotion to O-8 and also because the general and flag officer management offices typically have a greater degree of awareness of potentially adverse incidents involving O-7s than incidents involving officers at the pay grades of O-6 and below. The process also inherently considers less information, because adverse information that has already been considered by a prior selection and confirmation process need not be considered again. Thus, only adverse information pertaining to events that occurred during time in grade as an O-7, or pertaining to events that came to light during that time, are considered in the promotion process to O-8.

The combination of fewer people and fewer adverse events results in a considerably less onerous process.

Assignment and Promotion for O-9 and O-10

Figure 3.3 provides a graphic representation of the assignment and promotion process for officers at the pay grades of O-9 and O-10.

Because all O-9 and O-10 officers hold their rank in position, the process that considers adverse information is the process to nominate officers for assignment to every O-9 and O-10 position. Such nominations may or may not entail a promotion, as many officers serve in more than one assignment in each senior grade. As Figure 3.3 indicates, the process begins with an identified current or projected vacancy. In the case of joint positions, the process is initiated with a request for nomination (RFN) from the Joint Staff. An internal service process also identifies positions from which the incumbent is leaving and thus which need a new officer assigned. Typically the service chief, with the support of his GOMO, selects candidates. Once a candidate has been identified, for either an internal or for a joint position, the general and flag officer management office or, in the case of one service, the service IG office, initiates checks for adverse information from the offices and data systems indicated previously (e.g., NCIS, CIDC, or OSI; service EO/EEO; and the service IG, who subsequently checks the DoD IG). One service maintains a system of record checks on all active general officers, so as to expedite the process for officers considered for an assignment.

If adverse information is identified, the service chief will sometimes select a different candidate, prior to the need for any discussion external to the service. In each instance, the service secretary formally selects the candidate. When doing so, the service secretary is required to certify that the systems of records contain no adverse information and that there are no planned or ongoing inquiries, as per DoDI 1320.4. If a selected candidate has adverse information, the service secretary must indicate awareness of the adverse information and provide information about the adverse information.

Figure 3.3
Assignment and Promotion to O-9 and O-10

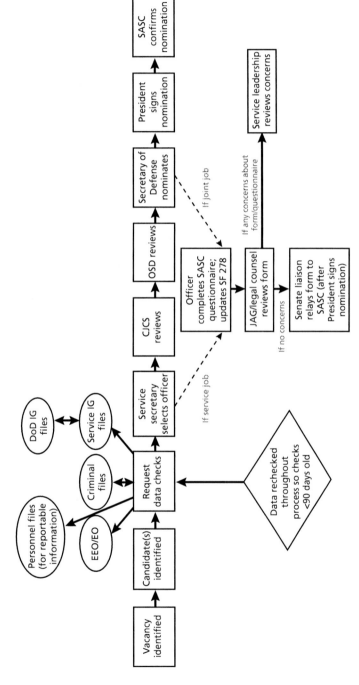

RAND MG1088-3.3

Individual officers nominated to O-9 or O-10 positions are required to complete a SASC questionnaire and to confirm that their personal SF 278 financial disclosure file is current. The services typically provide the questionnaire to the individual once the selection becomes apparent. When the individual is nominated for a service job, some services provide that paperwork to the individual after the service chief has made a final selection. Other services wait until the service secretary has signed the nomination. For joint positions, it is customary to wait until the Secretary of Defense has chosen from the candidates. Thus, Figure 3.3 indicates that the timing of when the officer completes the SASC questionnaire varies for a service position and a joint position. In every service, a legal officer verifies the consistency and acceptability of the questionnaire and SF 278 responses. In most cases, the service leadership does not always see the questionnaire and SF 278 responses. Instead, the completed SF 278 and SASC questionnaire are generally kept close-hold, and the legal officers forward any responses of concern to the service leadership. In those services, the service GOMO forwards the completed SASC questionnaire and SF 278 to OSD. The materials are subsequently sent to the SASC through liaison staff. However, in one service, the completed SASC questionnaire and SF 278 are routed through the general responsible for manpower and personnel issues, the chief of staff, and the service secretary before being sent to OSD and to the SASC through liaison staff.

The service secretary indicates his candidate selection with a nomination memorandum (also signed by the service chief[18]) that details the candidate's experience in combat or contingency operations and includes a paragraph that states:

All systems of records, to include Equal Employment Opportunity files and the Standard Form 278 (Public Financial Disclosure Report), maintained in the Department of Defense that pertain to this officer have been examined. The files contain no adverse information about this officer since his last Senate confirmation. Further, to the best of our knowledge, there is no

[18] CJCSI 1331.01D, p. D-6, notes that the service chief's signature is included as courtesy to the service chief.

planned or ongoing investigation or inquiry into matters that constitute alleged adverse information on the part of this officer. Further, Major General Public [sic] has not been implicated, nor is there any likelihood that he will be implicated in the Abu Ghraib prison abuse scandal.

The nomination is accompanied by the following, as per CJCSI 1331.01D:[19]

- current IG/DoD check, not more than 90 days old[20]
- certification of any connection to Abu Ghraib or detainee operations
- draft Secretary of Defense memorandum to the President
- White House scroll
- biography (both summary and full biography)
- press release
- photograph
- adverse information cover sheets, if applicable.
- time-in-position information.

For any initial appointment to O-9 or to O-10, the Chairman provides an evaluation of the officer's performance as a member of the Joint Staff or in other joint duty assignments.[21] This evaluation memorandum is included in the nomination packet.

The nomination packet proceeds from the Chairman to OUSD P&R for review, similar to that of the O-7 and O-8 lists.

---

[19]   This instruction does not specify which of these items are provided by the service and which are created in the Joint Staff before the package is forwarded to the Secretary of Defense, but these are generally generated by the service GOMO.

[20]   Note that this instruction does specify an IG/DoD check for O-9 and O-10 nominations, although the same instruction stated only the requirement for an IG check (not specifying IG/DoD) for actions involving O-7 and O-8 officers. The requirement was changed, from 60 days to 90, in August 2010 to be consistent with OSD requirements.

[21]   As per CJCSI 1331.01D, p. A-6.

As with other nominations, records checks are reinitiated every 60 days throughout this process to ensure that they are always less than 90 days old until the nomination is confirmed.

Retirement from General and Flag Officer Ranks

The retirement processes are illustrated in Figure 3.4.

Once an individual indicates an intent to retire, service personnel files, EEO files, criminal investigation, and IG files, as well as DoD IG files, must be checked within 60 days such that the service secretary can determine whether the officer served satisfactorily at that pay grade and is thus eligible for retirement from that pay grade. If there is potential adverse information from a pending investigation, the retirement decision is deferred so that the officer can be informed and the service secretary can obtain more information. Given information about the allegations being investigated and the anticipated date of completion, the service secretary is authorized to approve the retirement or defer the decision, based on the seriousness of the allegations, the likely outcome of the investigation, the needs of the service, and the personal situation of the officer.

Retirement from O-7 and O-8

The right side of Figure 3.4 has two different branches to indicate the different processes for retirement from O-7 and O-8, as contrasted with retirement from O-9 and O-10. The procedures for retirement from O-7 and O-8 are established by an October 9, 1998, Secretary of Defense memorandum, "Processing Retirement Applications of Officers in the Grades of O-7 and O-8." As the upper branch indicates, the service secretary or under secretary is authorized to determine that officers at the pay grades of O-7 and O-8 have served satisfactorily and thus are eligible for retirement at that grade, or that they have not, and

Figure 3.4
Retirement

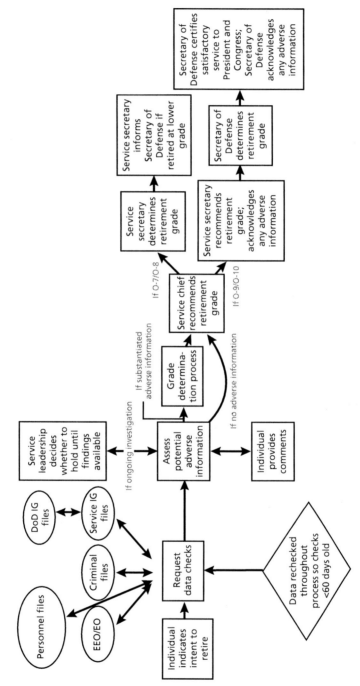

RAND *MG1088-3.4*

thus will be retired at a lower grade.[22] In the case of adverse information, the services initiate an internal grade determination process that
informs the officer and involves the input of individuals senior to the
officer under consideration. If a general or flag officer is retired at a
lower pay grade, the Secretary of Defense must be informed.[23] Additionally, USD P&R has the authority to approve a limited number of
TIG waivers for officers retiring from O-7 and O-8.

Retirement from O-9 and O-10

As shown in the lower branch on the right of Figure 3.4, the Secretary
of Defense is authorized to approve retirements from the pay grades of
O-9 and O-10. These processes are described in a June 1996 memorandum as well as in DoDI 1320.4.[24] In these instances, shown at the right
of Figure 3.4, the service secretary forwards the retirement recommendation to the Secretary of Defense, through the Chairman of the Joint
Chiefs of Staff, with a substantive explanation of why the Secretary of
Defense should certify that the officer has served satisfactorily in the
pay grade in which he or she is retiring. The retirement package must
indicate any adverse information or must make the standard certification (as per DoDI 1320.4) that there is no adverse information in the
DoD systems of records. If the retiring officer has adverse or alleged
misconduct that is identified prior to or during this process, then the
outcome of a service grade determination process is input to the service
secretary's recommendation to the Secretary of Defense regarding the
grade at which the individual should be retired.

At the request of the service secretary, the Secretary of Defense
may authorize a TIG waiver for an individual retiring at the pay grade
of O-9 or O-10 without sufficient time in grade. However, such waiv-

---

[22] This authorization assumes that officers have served a sufficient amount of time in grade.
If that is not the case, USD P&R is authorized to approve a limited annual number of TIG
waivers for O-7 and O-8.

[23] USD P&R, "Informing the Secretary of Downward Grade Adjustments," memorandum
for Assistant Secretary of the Army (Manpower and Reserve Affairs), Assistant Secretary of
the Navy (Manpower and Reserve Affairs), Assistant Secretary of the Air Force (Manpower
and Reserve Affairs), Washington, D.C., August 13, 2003.

[24] USD P&R, June 21, 1996.

ers may not be granted to individuals with ongoing investigations or potentially adverse information.

After the Secretary of Defense has approved the retirement, OSD informs the White House Military Office. Subsequently, OSD informs the SASC and also the service secretary that the retirement has been approved. However, the retirement is not yet complete.

Approximately 75 days prior to retirement, the service secretary must forward to the Secretary of Defense notice that there is no new adverse information that would affect the Secretary of Defense's approval and certification of the retirement to the President and to the Congress. This assurance must be forwarded from the Secretary of Defense to the President, the President of the Senate, and to the Speaker of the House of Representatives.[25] After the Secretary of Defense transmits these memoranda, the retirement may be publicly announced and may occur.[26]

Should adverse information be identified after the Secretary of Defense's announcement, the service secretary or the DoD IG must notify OSD within five days. The retirement nomination will be held in abeyance until the information is reviewed by the service, so that the service secretary can revise or maintain the service recommendation for retirement grade.

This process is different from the other personnel processes in that only adverse information is considered, rather than both adverse and reportable. Further, only adverse information from the current pay grade is of note, as the process is focused on satisfactory service in the current pay grade. Additionally, this process does not require Senate confirmation.

---

[25] While the order of events is upheld, the timeline is adjusted for retirements that are submitted within 60 days, as per USD P&R, June 21, 1996.

[26] If a service submits a retirement to OSD more than 75 days prior, the retirement may be approved, contingent upon the service secretary's recertification, at 75 days, that the retiring officer has no new adverse information.

Summary

In summary, the personnel processes of note include the selection and promotion process for O-7s and O-8s, the assignment and promotion nomination processes for O-9 and O-10, and the general and flag officer retirement process.

Regarding O-7 and O-8 selection and promotion processes, each service conducts the prescreenings by different offices, but the conduct of the prescreenings is similar, with a few exceptions.

There are inadequacies in the EO and EEO screenings and data to support those screenings, and not all the services are requesting screenings from the DoD IG prior to the O-7 selection board, or from the central clearance facility.

There are differences in the format of the adverse information provided to the selection boards, but it is unclear whether there are differences in the substantive detail provided.

The processes to identify adverse information from potentially adverse information also differ slightly, with two services employing in-person discussions and two services relying upon sequential review and approval by progressively more senior personnel.

Following the selection boards, each service responds to newly identified adverse information with PRBs, although the amount of information provided to the PRBs may vary.

In the case of the O-9 and O-10 assignment and promotion process, there are several differences among service processes. One difference is the extent to which data checks inform the selection of a potential candidate; one service maintains current data checks on all general officers, and one service will forward candidate names as far as the Chairman's office prior to receiving the results of the data inquiries. The remaining two services request data checks upon the occasion of a new candidate and consult the results of those checks prior to forwarding a candidate name to the Chairman's office.

Retirement processes for general and flag officers are conducted similarly in each service and vary from the other personnel processes discussed. These processes focus only on adverse information from the current pay grade of the retiring officer. Additionally, general and flag officer retirement does not require Senate confirmation.

CHAPTER FOUR

Evaluation and Discussion

Chapter Two described the services' processes that consider and evaluate possible adverse and reportable information in personnel processes for general and flag officers. This chapter discusses selected aspects of these processes further and identifies where our analysis indicates some gaps between requirements and actual practice.

DoD and Joint Staff Documented Guidance

There are several issues of concern with the DoD and Joint Staff documentation that describes the required processes. The first issue is that the DoD guidance requires formal update. DoDI 1320.4 is dated March 1995 and is supplemented by memoranda, including the February 27, 2002, memorandum that changes the requirement from DoD IG checks from 60 days current to 90 days current; the July 19, 2006, memorandum that requires selection boards to consider adverse information; and the February 12, 2007, memorandum regarding exemplary conduct. These memoranda permit flexible adjustments to the required processes, but copies must be acquired from others expert in the processes; the memoranda are not readily available.

Throughout the instructions and memoranda, there exists no clear definition of reportable information. DoDI 1320.4 states,

> Normally, the Department of Defense does not report alleged adverse information or other unsubstantiated allegations to the Senate. However, in extraordinary cases, such as where the alle-

33

gations received significant media attention or when the Senate Armed Service Committee (SASC) brings allegations to the attention of the Department of Defense, the Secretaries of the Military Departments shall include a discussion of the unsubstantiated allegations in the nomination package.

Such information would be reportable. Mention of reportable information also appears in CJCSI 1331.01D. That instruction calls out one particular type of reportable information when it requires nominee packages to include "certification as to any connection to Abu Ghraib or detainee operations" but does not use the term "reportable" and does not mention other kinds of reportable information. Further, while reportable information is currently treated as a category of information, or a list of events, there is no clear explanation of how reportable information is added or deleted. Further, there is no specification of how precise the definition of reportable events need be or what proximity to the event or events is required. For example, if an officer had no immediate involvement with detainee operations, but does serve in the chain of command for personnel in detainee operations, service personnel question whether this constitutes reportable information. At the extreme, the combatant command (COCOM) commander is in the chain of command for detainee operations; is this reportable information for the COCOM commander? Likewise, when a particular occurrence, such as operations in Haditha or Hamandaya, attracts media attention and is subsequently noted as reportable, service personnel do not understand the proximity to those issues required before information is reportable. For example, if a general officer commanded a unit in Haditha or Hamandaya other than the unit that incurred media attention, is that command considered reportable information?

There are also several ways that the DoD and CJCS guidance are unclear about the data checks required for processing nominations. DoDI 1320.4 specifically mentions EEO but not EO when it states "The Secretaries of the Military Departments shall ensure that all investigative files, to include Equal Employment Opportunity files, are reviewed prior to forwarding a nomination to the Secretary of Defense." While this statement is inclusive of EO when referencing "all investigative files," specific mention of EO would help ensure recognition that EEO and EO are different, and that both are relevant.

Another instruction that provides inconsistent guidance is CJCSI 1331.01D. This instruction was updated in August 2010 to be consistent with the OSD requirement for IG checks on nominees to be not more than 90 days old. However, while this instruction states that the Secretary of Defense requires a current IG check on all nominees, it does not specify for O-7s and O-8s whether the IG check can be from the service IG or whether it must be from the DoD IG. Likewise, DoDI 1320.4 may also require modification regarding the data checks. It states only that the DoD IG check must be renewed. The current practice is to ensure that all data checks are renewed, but the instruction does not require those renewals.

Services' Processes and Guidance

The services' processes, and the offices involved in the process, differ regarding the roles of the offices involved. However, as long as adverse and reportable information are managed consistently across the services, there appears to be no compelling reason that the services' processes or offices involved should be the same.

There are some shortcomings to the service-specific guidance. While several services have well-detailed service-specific guidance regarding some of the processes discussed herein, either in the form of memoranda or service instructions, no service has detailed guidance pertaining to all the processes described in this monograph. Related to this, no single office or individual in any service is responsible for the consideration of adverse information during the assignment, promotion, and retirement processes. Oversight of these processes occurs in multiple offices, including those offices that manage O-6s, as well as the general and flag officer management offices, IG, criminal investigative offices, EO and EEO offices, JAG, and general counsel offices. As a result, although each service had individuals expert in parts of the process, no single individual in any service was expert in the entire process and the relevant data. This makes it very difficult for the services to assess their own overall processes and will also likely complicate any effort to establish more complete service-specific guidance.

EEO/EO Processes and Data

The preceding chapter's discussion of assignment and promotion practices suggested some shortcomings in the extent to which EEO and EO data are being considered. The discussion of these shortcomings appears here, as an alternative to diverting from the overall discussion of the assignment and promotion practices in the earlier chapter. Thus, this section includes both a description of the processes and an evaluation of the current practices.

First, to understand the processes the services and OSD undertake to check EO and EEO files, it is necessary to understand the differences between the two terms and the regulations and procedures that apply to each.

Within DoD, allegations of discrimination brought by service members are called "equal opportunity (EO)" complaints, or sometimes "military equal opportunity (MEO)" complaints.[1] In contrast, the term "equal employment opportunity (EEO)" applies to allegations brought by civilians.[2] It is the employment status of the person making the allegation that determines the path a complaint takes and therefore whether the EO or EEO procedure applies. Hence, a general or flag officer may be implicated in either an EEO or an EO complaint, depending on the status of the person making the allegation.

Handling of EO Complaints

By DoD directive,[3] the services handle EO complaints—those brought by military members—through command channels. Investigations of EO complaints are conducted through either a commander's or an IG investigation. All the services maintain military EO counselors and a formal EO structure at all levels of command. These organizations conduct EO training and maintain EO awareness. Further, unit- and

---

[1]   Department of Defense Directive (DoDD) 1350.2, *Department of Defense Military Equal Opportunity (MEO) Program*, August 18, 1995, certified current as of November 21, 2003.

[2]   DoDD 1440.1, *The DoD Civilian Equal Employment Opportunity (EEO) Program*, May 21, 1987, certified current as of November 21, 2003.

[3]   DoDD 1350.2.

installation-level counselors' responsibilities entail striving to equitably resolve allegations of discrimination before a formal EO complaint is filed. Service regulations require formal EO complaints implicating a general or flag officer to be handled by an IG investigation rather than a commander's investigation.[4] Ultimately, military members have the right to appeal a decision on a formal EO complaint by filing a discrimination suit in federal district court.

Handling of EEO Complaints

EEO complaints—those brought by civilian employees or applicants— are handled through a completely separate process from EO complaints. The EEO process is governed by separate laws and regulations.[5] In fact, DoDD 1440.1 requires EO and EEO programs at each installation to be managed by military and civilian personnel, respectively, and to serve only their respective populations.[6] EEO investigations are conducted outside the chain of command, relying instead on an EEO-specific process that begins with informal inquiries, the possibility of mediation, and then, if necessary, resolution in EEO-specific channels overseen by the Equal Employment Opportunity Commission (EEOC). As with EO, all the services and DoD maintain EEO organizations and policies at all levels of command, from individual installations to departmental headquarters. This is in part because the various EEO-related laws and implementing regulations require them to exist.

If an informal, preliminary ("pre-complaint") settlement process does not resolve an EEO allegation,[7] a formal complaint phase is

---

[4]   See U.S. Department of the Army, *Army Command Policy*, AR 600-20, June 7, 2006, paragraph D-2,c; U.S. Department of the Navy, *Naval Equal Opportunity (EO) Policy*, OPNAVINST 5354.1F, July 25, 2007, paragraph 7,k,(19); U.S. Department of the Air Force, *Inspector General Complaints Resolution*, AFI 90-301, May 15, 2008, paragraph 3.2.1.1.

[5]   See 29 C.F.R. 1614.103, which specifically excludes uniformed military personnel from applicability in EEO complaints of discrimination.

[6]   DoDD 1440.1, paragraph 5.2.15.

[7]   Local EEO counselors typically handle the pre-complaint phase, seeking to resolve a complaint either through counseling or an alternate dispute resolution process, such as mediation (U.S. Equal Employment Opportunity Commission, "Overview Of Federal Sector EEO Complaint Process," web page, undated).

initiated and the investigation is turned over to the Civilian Personnel Management Service (CPMS), a DoD agency that conducts such investigations; the military departments do not conduct formal EEO investigations.[8] Upon completion of an investigation, the complainant may either request a hearing before an EEOC administrative judge or challenge the decision in federal district court.

An EEO complainant normally brings allegations against the relevant government agency, but may also name a responsible management official (RMO) in that organization. The RMO is the person the complainant perceives as having personally discriminated against the complainant. In addition, commanders at any level and agency heads, such as the Secretary of the Army or the Secretary of Defense, may be named by virtue of their position rather than any personal act of discrimination.

EO and EEO Databases

All services collect, maintain, and report statistical data on the number of EEO and EO complaints, but searchable investigative databases are neither universal nor complete. The available data resources are discussed below.

Due to the decentralized authority given to commanders to investigate EO complaints though command channels, the extent of centralized investigative databases recording EO cases varies across the services. Two services maintain a comprehensive database of all formal EO complaints, and a third service is developing such a database. The fourth service has not yet undertaken to build one. But because IGs conduct EO investigations involving general and flag officers, IG files provide a reliable source of records of such investigations. For EO investigations involving officers of lower grades, there exist no comparable databases, either in the services or OSD. In one service, commanders' investigations involving officers in the grade of major or above are reported to the IG and records are maintained in an IG database.

---

[8]   DoDD 5505.06, *Investigations of Allegations Against Senior Officials of the Department of Defense*, April 10, 2006, does authorize the DoD IG to conduct parallel investigations of acts of personal discrimination by senior officials.

Due to the more centralized nature of EEO investigations and the more extensive set of formal regulations, EEO databases tend to be more comprehensive than EO databases. Yet, there is still some variability across services. Three services maintain centralized EEO databases, but one keeps files on all active formal EEO cases; one of the three maintains centralized records of both pre-complaint and formal investigations; the fourth service is developing a centralized database.

EO and EEO Record Checks Pursuant to Promotions, Appointments, and Retirement

DoDD 1320.4 requires the secretaries of the military departments to ensure that "all investigative files, to include EEO files, are reviewed prior to forwarding a nomination to the Secretary of Defense for general and flag officer actions requiring approval by the Secretary of Defense or the President, or confirmation by the Senate." Because the regulation specifically calls out EEO and leaves EO unnamed and covered under the umbrella of "all investigative files," there appears to be a lack of clarity within the services as to the need to check both EEO and EO investigative files.

Two services check with their respective EEO offices but not their EO offices; one of those two services was erroneously checking the EEO office that kept records only on headquarters personnel rather than on the entire service. That has now been corrected. One service checks both EO and EEO files; when its GOMO requests an EEO check, the EEO office queries every field location to check all the nominees' names against all current EEO cases, thereby providing an up-to-date comprehensive EEO file check. The fourth service checks its EO office but not its EEO office, but neither the EO nor the EEO office in that service maintains a comprehensive investigative database. Further, that service conducts only post-board checks, not pre-board checks. The other three services conduct checks both times.

Evaluation of EO and EEO Checks as Part of the Assignment and Promotion Processes

The EO and EEO file check processes are uneven. Because IGs investigate EO complaints involving general and flag officers and are notified of EEO cases against such officers, the service checks with IGs provide a fairly reliable source of information. Nevertheless, one problem is that a general or flag officer could be implicated in a case without being named the RMO. This is recognized in one service, where an IG staff person scours all EO and EEO investigations reported to that IG office for any general or flag officer implications, even if the officer was not named the RMO. This entails reading the entire report and supporting documents. Interviewees from all the services complain about the inability to electronically search EO and EEO files by name to ensure that no nominee's name is missed either in the narrative of the investigative report or in attachments.

Finally, there are potential reporting gaps on any investigations that may have occurred while officers were in lower grades but within the ten-year window. One service closes this gap by requiring reports to the IG on all such investigations on majors and above. This policy would include most, or all, of the ten-year window.

Representatives of three of the four services report concern about the lack of comprehensiveness of the EO and EEO file-check processes. These concerns appear to be justified due to uneven recordkeeping policies and the gap due to lack of IG records on officers earlier in their careers, as mentioned above.

DoD IG Screens

DoDI 1320.4, as modified by the July 19, 2006, USD P&R memorandum, requires a DoD IG check for each eligible officer prior to the promotion selection boards and for each nominee following the selection boards. This research found that these DoD IG checks were inconsistently requested among the services. Three services have explicit guidance to conduct these checks, including the check for eligible officers prior to the selection board. All services have been conducting DoD IG checks prior to the O-8 selection boards. However, only two services were requesting DoD IG checks prior to the O-7 selection board.

All agree that requesting and conducting both service IG and DoD IG prescreens for all officers eligible for O-7 is arduous. This is due to the large numbers of O-6s considered eligible for selection and promotion to O-7. Many of these officers are considered very unlikely to be promoted, including those officers that have not been selected for many years.

Some service personnel also maintain that the DoD IG checks are unnecessary. Those who believe this to be the case typically explain that DoD IG does not investigate officers at the pay grades of O-6 or below. As a result, they are likely to know about investigations of these officers only when a complaint is made directly to the DoD IG hotline. In these instances, the DoD IG refers the complaint to the service IG to investigate. The service IG provides the DoD IG with the resolution when the investigation is complete. As a result, the DoD IG should only have information on officers at pay grades of O-6 and below that the service IG already possesses. This would suggest that the DoD IG checks are redundant with the service IG checks. However, one service, which has been consistently requesting DoD IG checks for officers eligible to O-7, reports that it has received information from the DoD IG for these eligible officers that was not available from its service IG. In other words, the DoD IG checks have inexplicably provided new information and thus do not appear to be completely redundant with service IG checks.

The lack of DoD IG checks for all O-7 eligible officers prior to the selection board is an unacceptable deviation from the requirement. However, it appears that service processes have been adjusted such that all services will be conducting DoD IG checks prior to subsequent O-7 and O-8 selection boards.

The Amount of Detail Provided to Selection Boards and Promotion Review Boards

SASC staff feel strongly that the best individuals to consider the merit of an officer with adverse information are uniformed officers. Thus, SASC staff advocate the current practice of providing adverse information to promotion selection boards for their consideration, rather than subsequently providing the information only for Senate consideration.

However, the promotion selection boards see only a very brief summary (typically one page) of the adverse information. Some involved in the process have suggested that those summaries are subjective, in that the summary can be written to minimize or deemphasize the adverse nature of the individual case. When the adverse information is not available for the selection board, a PRB is convened to address adverse information for recent selectees. In these instances, the amount of information provided to the PRB varies. One service provides the members of the PRB with the complete investigative materials, which typically fill several binders. One service now provides a redacted ROI (typically seven to ten pages of information), along with the officer's input and the command response to the incident.[9] Another service decides on a case-by-case basis of whether to provide a redacted ROI or a one-page summary.

SASC staff interviewed for this effort suggest that shorter summaries may disadvantage the officer by not providing the ameliorating circumstances. Some service representatives believe that longer summaries burden the selection boards and disadvantage the individual officers with adverse information. This research did not conclude whether more information provided to the selection board would advantage or disadvantage the officer. However, having varying amounts of information provided to the selection boards suggests inconsistencies across the service promotion processes. Likewise, having both different amounts of information and also different types (e.g., redacted or complete) of information provided to PRBs also suggests a problematic inconsistency. Given that the purpose of the PRB is to advise the service secretary whether to continue to support the promotion, the PRB should have privileged access to the complete case materials, as are available to the service secretary. However, all but one service state concerns about providing complete (i.e, unredacted) investigation materials.

---

[9]   This service has previously provided only a one-page summary of the information to the PRB.

Greater Focus on Assignment and Promotion Processes Than on Retirement

This monograph addresses the consideration of adverse and reportable information in both assignment and promotion processes and also in retirement processes for general and flag officers. However, SASC and DoD concerns appear to be more focused on assignment and promotion processes than on the retirement processes. Formerly, Senate confirmation was required for general and flag officer retirements. As of the 1996 National Defense Authorization Act,[10] officers can be retired after the Secretary of Defense certifies in writing to the President and the Congress that the officer has served satisfactorily in grade. This delegation from Congress to DoD suggests a lower priority for Congress. Additionally, retirement requires only a certification that the officer has served satisfactorily while in that grade. This is a shorter period of consideration than would apply were the same officer being promoted or assigned. The focus on assignment and promotion rather than retirement is not problematic, but it is noted here as explanation of why the discussion herein focuses primarily on the assignment and promotion processes.

DoD and the SASC Have Different Philosophies

DoD and the SASC appear to bring different philosophies to these processes, and thus perceive the processes and, on occasion the outcomes, differently.[11] This observation is included herein not for evaluation, but because an understanding of these differences may increase the effectiveness of communication between DoD and the SASC.

The differences in their perspectives are evident in several ways. First, their overall focus differs. DoD tends to regard adverse information as pertaining to an incident, or an investigation of an incident.

---

[10]   Public Law 104-106.

[11]   Throughout this monograph, references to the SASC refer to those SASC staff with whom we met and discussed these issues.

With this framework, DoD is thus able to evaluate adverse information against regulations and standards, such as standards of conduct or misconduct. The SASC considers adverse information in a way that is subtly different; our interviews with SASC staff suggest that they are interested more in the entirety of an individual, including (and especially) that individual's judgment. This becomes problematic, because not only are IG investigations (one of the primary sources of adverse information) not intended to evaluate an individual's judgment, but they are explicitly instructed not to assess judgment.

This difference in perspective explains how a service and the SASC can view a single individual differently. The service might claim that an individual does not have adverse information, because an IG investigation found the allegation was unsubstantiated. However, the SASC might focus on the content of investigation and assert that the individual's judgment was questionable. For example, if a senior officer is found to be more lenient to officers than to enlisted personnel (guilty of the same offense), the IG might claim that the officer was within his or her authority to respond to those incidents as he or she chose. Nonetheless, the SASC might assert that such responses suggest a bias that indicates poor judgment.

Within the services, the only official assessment of judgment occurs in the officer's evaluation report. In some instances, judgment lapses are counseled through unofficial or private communication, such as the Marine Corps non-punitive letter of communication (NPLC). However, these documents are not included in documentation for personnel processes. In the case of NPLCs or other private communication, the services are inclined to assert that the counseling and any subsequent command actions were sufficient consequence for the judgment lapse that incurred the counseling. The SASC is more inclined to think that even incidents that were treated privately should be considered in the promotion of more senior officers, and the SASC is inclined to grant less discretion to the most senior officers.

In contrast, the services adamantly assert that commanders should have the opportunity to counsel officers without the incident or the counseling being included in a future nomination package, or being requested by the SASC in the event of a nomination.[12] Otherwise, senior officers may be reticent to counsel and develop their subordinates properly, for fear that minor, informal counseling could later have disproportionate consequences.

These differences illustrate that DoD and the SASC differ in general regarding the threshold of information that should be considered during personnel processes. Another difference is that the SASC would apply different standards for different pay grades. The SASC perspective would suggest that a minor adverse incident may be insufficient to preclude nomination to the pay grade of O-7 but that the same incident could preclude nomination for promotion to the pay grade of O-10 for another individual or even, subsequently, for the same individual. A system that employed different thresholds of information for different ranks would be less forgiving of mistakes and "learning opportunities" among more senior officers by applying increased scrutiny with rank. The current system does not apply such increased scrutiny. Instead, the current system applies scrutiny to individual incidents consistently regardless of rank. Further, the current system does not revisit adverse information. In other words, if an individual receives a nomination despite adverse information, that same adverse information is not considered during subsequent nomination processes.

DoD and the SASC also differ in the duration of interest regarding adverse information. DoDI 1320.4, as modified by the July 19, 2006, memorandum, defines adverse information, in part, as being less than ten years old. However, when individuals complete the SASC questionnaire, they are asked about potential adverse incidents without any time restrictions.

One additional difference between DoD and the SASC pertains to the amount of study accorded to individual cases with adverse or potentially adverse information. SASC staff report instances in which, after reading investigative files or other materials sent to them in support of a nomination, they suspected that DoD personnel had not read the files before sending them. While SASC staff assert that service

---

[12] There is no evidence that adverse information is being inappropriately handled through private counseling.

representatives should read each case in its entirety, service personnel acknowledge that they do not read each complete investigative file. They maintain that while some cases do require a careful reading of all supporting materials, others appear self-evident even from the investigative summary. In many, or even most, cases, the service personnel read the entire IG investigative report but do not read the supporting files.

There have been instances in which SASC staff have read portions of the investigative files and raised additional concerns regarding the nominee. We suggest, however, that even when DoD personnel have read the entire file, they may not react with concern to the same excerpted material. The overlying difference in philosophy may explain why SASC staff would react negatively to material that might, to them, suggest questionable judgment, whereas service representatives are less likely to read the files as a portrayal of the nominee's character. Instead, as mentioned earlier, service personnel are more likely to see the investigations as supporting a decision that an allegation is either substantiated or not substantiated, as measured against defined regulations.

CHAPTER FIVE

Recommendations

This chapter provides the recommendations that emerge from this research and the observations discussed in the prior chapter.

OSD and the Joint Staff should update DoD and Joint Staff guidance. Given the finding that DoD and Joint Staff guidance are outdated, lack a clear definition of reportable information, are inconsistent with one another, and convey guidance through a set of instructions and memoranda, this study recommends the updating of these guidance documents. This is especially necessary given that key aspects of the DoD guidance are included in memoranda (e.g., February 27, 2002, and July 19, 2006) that do not appear in centralized DoD databases. The February 27, 2002, memorandum refers to forthcoming updates of DoDI 1320.4, but these updates have not occurred. Further, the Chairman's instructions should be consistent with the revised DoD instructions.

When the DoD guidance is updated, the revised instruction should clarify the definition of reportable information and the means by which the list of reportable information will be updated and distributed to the general and flag officer management offices. One of the complicating factors when interpreting reportable information guidance is the proximity required to the event—for example, the levels of command or the geographic proximity to an event that would make an individual of interest, or his or her experiences reportable. Thus, the guidance should, to the extent possible, require reportable topics to clarify the involvement required for reportable information. Additionally, the guidance would ideally specify that, when adding to the list of issues that qualify as reportable information, there must be a date at which that issue will be removed from the list, absent further action to retain that issue on the list. Alternatively, reportable information could be treated like adverse information, in that once adverse information is considered for a particular officer, that information is not reconsidered for the next nomination. Such a policy would, for example, have negated the need to continue mentioning involvement in the 1991 Tailhook convention in recent nominations of Navy admirals.

The services should clarify, with formal service directives or instructions, the processes by which adverse information is considered in general and flag officer personnel processes. Secretary of the Navy Instruction (SECNAVINST) 1401.4A, and the Secretary of the Navy's March 1, 1998, memorandum for the Adverse Material Advisory Board are both good examples of service guidance for individual processes—in these examples, the consideration of adverse information by selection boards and the process to assess whether information is adverse, respectively.[1] Additionally, the Army memorandum that describes the process for O-7 and O-8 promotion is also an excellent resource.[2] However, there should be specific service instructions that pertain to the consideration of adverse information both preceding and following selection boards, and during the assignment and promotion processes for officers at O-9 and O-10.

Given the finding that no service had a single individual or office who was responsible for, or expert in, the entire process, **each service should identify the office responsible for the entire nomination and retirement process, including the inclusion of adverse and reportable information.** While the processes involve resources and

---

[1]   Secretary of the Navy Instruction 1401.4A, *Consideration of Credible Information of an Adverse Nature by General and Flag Officer Selection Boards*, February 14, 2007; Secretary of the Navy, "Instructions for Conduct of the Adverse Material Advisory Board (AMAB)," memorandum for Adverse Material Advisory Board, Washington, D.C., March 1, 1998.

[2]   U.S. Department of the Army, Secretary of the Army, "Policy Concerning Adverse Information for Officers Being Considered for Promotion, Appointment, or Federal Recognition to a General Officer Grade," memorandum, January 22, 2007. Not available to the general public.

individuals representing various service offices (e.g., service secretary, chief of staff, general officer or senior leader management, IG, JAG), there should be an individual who bears overall responsibility and has full awareness of the processes, data, and time line involved.

The services should ensure that they satisfy the requirement to prescreen all officers eligible for promotion to pay grades O-7 and O-8 and that the prescreens include DoD IG checks as well as EO and EEO checks. The service data should support the EO and EEO checks.

The services should provide a consistent and sufficient amount of detail to the promotion selection boards regarding adverse information. This recommendation acknowledges that the time constraints of the selection boards preclude them from considering detailed depictions of adverse information. However, selection boards should view an objective characterization of adverse information with a reasonable amount of detail to convey the circumstances. A review by OSD regarding the amount of information provided to the selection boards may be warranted.

The services should provide complete investigative materials to promotion review boards. The members of a PRB are senior, trusted officers, and they should be entrusted to view the complete investigative materials in order to provide their best counsel to the service secretary.

Law and regulations should retain the opportunity for the services to privately counsel officers without risk of the incident being considered in a nomination. Many service representatives, including general and flag officers, interviewed for this study adamantly assert that commanders should have the opportunity to counsel officers without the incident, or the counseling, being included in a future nomination package or being requested by the SASC in the event of a nomination. Otherwise, senior officers may be reticent to counsel and develop their subordinates properly, for fear that minor, informal counseling could later have disproportionate consequences. This study found no evidence that adverse information is inappropriately handled through private counseling. However, the services should recognize this opportunity as a privilege and recognize that this privilege could be lost if the SASC identifies any cases in which adverse information was inappropriately handled through private counseling.

The SASC and DoD should initiate a dialog and recognize the differences between the DoD and SASC perspectives regarding adverse information processes, especially pertaining to levels of scrutiny and issues of individual judgment. An increased understanding of the SASC perspective should inform DoD interaction with the SASC during nomination processes.

Service personnel should explicitly determine which individual cases do *not* require a complete reading of the investigative materials. This is a subtly different from the current process. While this approach would not result in complete readings of all cases, it would result in a complete reading of more cases. In contrast to the current practice of deciding which cases *do* require a complete reading, this approach would change the default assumption and thus would exempt from complete assessment only those cases that are clearly self-evident.

Bibliography

Assistant Secretary of Defense for Force Management Policy, "Interim Change to Department of Defense Instruction (DoDI) 1320.4, 'Military Officer Actions Requiring Approval of the Secretary of Defense or President, or Confirmation by the Senate,'" memorandum for Secretary of the Army, Secretary of the Navy, Secretary of the Air Force, Chairman of the Joint Chiefs of Staff, Washington, D.C., February 27, 2002.

———, "Processing Three- and Four-Star Retirement Requests," memorandum for Acting Secretary of the Army, Acting Secretary of the Navy, Acting Secretary of the Air Force, Chairman of the Joint Chiefs of Staff, Washington, D.C., May 21, 2001.

Chairman of the Joint Chiefs of Staff Instruction 1330.02A, *Review of Promotion Selection Board Results by the Chairman of the Joint Chiefs of Staff*, May 1, 1997.

Chairman of the Joint Chiefs of Staff Instruction 1331.01D, *Manpower and Personnel Actions Involving General and Flag Officers*, August 2010.

CJCSI—*See* Chairman of the Joint Chiefs of Staff Instruction.

DoDD—*See* U.S. Department of Defense Directive.

DoDI—*See* U.S. Department of Defense Instruction.

Public Law 104-106, Fiscal Year 1996 National Defense Authorization Act, February 10, 1996.

Public Law 109-163, Fiscal Year 2006 National Defense Authorization Act, January 6, 2006.

Secretary of Defense, "General and Flag Officer Nominations," memorandum for the Secretary of the Army, Washington, D.C., September 2, 1988.

———, "Processing Retirement Applications of Officers in the Grades of O-7 and O-8," memorandum for Secretary of the Army, Secretary of the Navy, Secretary of the Air Force, Undersecretary of Defense (Personnel and Readiness), General Counsel (DoD), Inspector General (DoD), Washington, D.C., October 19, 1998.

————, "Three- and Four-Star Retirement Approval," memorandum for Secretary of the Army, Secretary of the Navy, Secretary of the Air Force, Chairman of the Joint Chiefs of Staff, Under Secretary of Defense for Personnel and Readiness, Washington, D.C., August 17, 2002.

————, "Delegation of Authority Pertaining to the Retirement of Officers Under Title 10 United States Code, Section 1370," memorandum for Secretaries of the Military Departments, Chairman of the Joint Chiefs of Staff, Under Secretary of Defense for Personnel and Readiness, Washington, D.C., June 5, 2003.

Secretary of the Navy, "Instructions for Conduct of the Adverse Material Advisory Board (AMAB)," memorandum for Adverse Material Advisory Board, Washington, D.C., March 1, 1998.

Secretary of the Navy Instruction 1401.4A, *Consideration of Credible Information of an Adverse Nature by General and Flag Officer Selection Boards*, February 14, 2007.

Secretary of the Navy Instruction 1420.1B, *Promotion, Special Selection, Selective Early Retirement, and Selective Early Removal Boards for Commissioned Officers of the Navy and Marine Corps*, March 28, 2006.

Secretary of the Navy Instruction 1920.6C CH-1, *Administrative Separation of Officers*, September 19, 2007.

Under Secretary of Defense for Personnel and Readiness, "Memorandum Provides Instructions for the Processing of Three- and Four-Star Retirement Recommendations," memorandum for Secretary of the Army, Secretary of the Navy, Secretary of the Air Force, Chairman of the Joint Chiefs of Staff, Washington, D.C., June 21, 1996.

————, "Managing Adverse Information," memorandum for the Deputy Secretary of Defense, Washington, D.C., January 31, 2003.

————, "Informing the Secretary of Downward Grade Adjustments," memorandum for Assistant Secretary of the Army (Manpower and Reserve Affairs), Assistant Secretary of the Navy (Manpower and Reserve Affairs), Assistant Secretary of the Air Force (Manpower and Reserve Affairs), Washington, D.C., August 13, 2003.

————, "General and Flag Officer Boards—Adverse Information of a Credible Nature," memorandum for Secretary of the Army, Secretary of the Navy, Secretary of the Air Force, Chairman of the Joint Chiefs of Staff, Washington, D.C., July 19, 2006.

————, "Officer Appointments—Exemplary Conduct," memorandum for Secretary of the Army, Secretary of the Navy, Secretary of the Air Force, Chairman of the Joint Chiefs of Staff, Washington, D.C., February 12, 2007.

U.S. Department of the Air Force, *Military Equal Opportunity*, AFI 36-2706, July 29, 2004.

————, *Equal Employment Opportunity Complaints*, AFI 36-1201, February 12, 2008.

————, *Inspector General Complaints Resolution*, AFI 90-301, May 15, 2008.

————, *Officer Promotions and Selective Continuation*, **AFI** 36-2501, August 17, 2009.

————, *Service Retirements*, AFI 36-2303, December 10, 2009.

U.S. Department of the Air Force, Secretary of the Air Force, "SOUIF Decision Policy," memorandum, July 22, 2005.

————, "Air Force Equal Opportunity," memorandum, April 23, 2009.

U.S. Department of the Army, *Equal Employment Opportunity and Affirmative Action*, AR 690-12, March 4, 1988.

————, *Unit Equal Opportunity Training Guide*, DA Pamphlet 350-20, June 1, 1994.

————, *Army Grade Determination Review Board and Grade Determinations*, AR 15-80, July 12, 2002.

————, *Equal Employment Opportunity Complaints*, AR 690-600, February 9, 2004.

————, "Policies and Procedures for Active-Duty List Officer Selection Boards," DA Memorandum 600-2, February 9, 2004.

————, "Policies and Procedures for Reserve Components Officer Selection Boards," DA Memorandum 600-4, February 9, 2004.

————, *Officer Promotions*," AR 600-8-29, February 25, 2005.

————, *Army Command Policy*, AR 600-20, June 7, 2006.

————, *Procedures for Investigating Officers and Boards of Officers*, AR 15-5, October 2, 2006.

————, *Inspector General Activities and Procedures*, AR 20-1, February 1, 2007.

U.S. Department of the Army, Secretary of the Army, "Policy Concerning Adverse Information for Officers Being Considered for Promotion, Appointment, or Federal Recognition to a General Officer Grade," memorandum, January 22, 2007. Not available to the general public.

U.S. Department of Defense Directive 1350.2, *Department of Defense Military Equal Opportunity (MEO) Program*, August 18, 1995, certified current as of November 21, 2003.

U.S. Department of Defense Directive 1440.1, *The DoD Civilian Equal Employment Opportunity (EEO) Program*, May 21, 1987, certified current as of November 21, 2003.

U.S. Department of Defense Directive 5505.06, *Investigations of Allegations Against Senior Officials of the Department of Defense*, April 10, 2006.

U.S. Department of Defense Instruction 1320.14, *Commissioned Officer Promotion Program Procedures*, September 24, 1996.

U.S. Department of Defense Instruction 1320.4, *Military Officer Actions Requiring Approval of the Secretary of Defense or the President, or Confirmation by the Senate*, March 14, 1995.

U.S. Department of the Navy, *Naval Equal Opportunity (EO) Policy*, OPNAVINST 5354.1F, July 25, 2007.

U.S. Equal Employment Opportunity Commission, "Overview Of Federal Sector EEO Complaint Process," web page, undated. As of March 16, 2011: http://www.eeoc.gov/federal/fed_employees/complaint_overview.cfm

U.S. Senate, Committee on Armed Services, "Letter to the Honorable Frank Carlucci," signed by Sam Nunn and John W. Warner, Washington, D.C., August 1, 1988.

USD P&R—*See* Under Secretary of Defense for Personnel and Readiness.